TREASURES FROM THE PAST

TREASURES FROM SPAIN

David & Patricia Armentrout

The Rourke Book Company, Inc.
Vero Beach, Florida 32964

PHOTO CREDITS:
©Elwin Trump: cover, pages 31, 34, 37, 41; ©Al Michaud: pages 6, 16; ©Galyn C. Hammond: pages 12,
14, 26, 28; ©Corel Corporation: pages 18, 21, 24, 40, 43; ©Artville, LLC.: pages 4, 30; ©Gisela
Walberg/University of Cincinnati: page 9; ©PhotoDisc page 35

PRODUCED & DESIGNED by East Coast Studios
eastcoaststudios.com

EDITORIAL SERVICES:
Pamela Schroeder

Library of Congress Cataloging-in-Publication Data

Armentrout, David, 1962-
    Spain / David and Patricia Armentrout.
        p. cm. — (Treasures from the past)
    Includes bibliographical references and index.
    ISBN 1-55916-293-7
    1. Spain—Antiquities—Juvenile literature. 2. Excavations (Archaeology)—Spain—Juvenile literature. [1. Spain—
Antiquities. 2. Archaeology.] I. Armentrout, Patricia, 1960- II. Title. III. Treasures from the past (Vero Beach, Fla.)

DP44 .A73 2000
936.6—dc21

                                                                00–029076

Printed in the USA

TABLE OF CONTENTS

Learning About the Past

What will people who live 100 years from now think about us? Will they know anything about us? Will they know what was important, or valuable, to us? Will people be interested in learning about their **ancestors**? The answer is probably yes. People have always been interested in history. Most of us are curious about ancient civilizations. We find it amazing how ancient people lived their lives, how they struggled through hard times, and how they did so much with so little.

*A*ncient castles are among the buildings archaeologists study.
This castle is in Toledo in central Spain.

TIMELINE

1500 – 800 BC	Bronze Age begins in Spain. Greeks settle the Spanish coast.
800 BC – AD 300	Eastern Mediterranean people called Phoenicians settle and take over parts of Spain.
300 BC – AD 406	Most of Spain is ruled by the Roman Empire.
AD 406 – 700	Roman rule ends. Visigoths settle and rule Spain. Visigoth capital is Toledo.
AD 700 – 1000	Moors rule much of Spain.
AD 785	Great Mosque in Cordoba is built.
AD 1000 – 1400	Christians rule much of Spain. Seville Cathedral is built in 1402.
AD 1400 – 1600	Spanish galleons are used as warships and to haul cargo for trade. Spanish explorers discover and lay claim to several areas in South America.
AD 1492	Christopher Columbus sails to the New World. Moorish rule ends in Spain.
AD 1500	Tobacco smoking is introduced to Spain.
AD 1503	Spain approves slavery in American colonies.
AD 1506	Christopher Columbus dies.
AD 1519 – 1521	Hernan Cortes meets Aztec ruler Montezuma and conquers the Aztec capital Tenochtitlan.
AD 1561	Madrid is capital of Spain.

How do we learn about the past? It's fairly easy to learn about recent history. Much of what has happened in the past 100 years has been recorded in books and newspapers and in radio and television broadcasts. We have many examples of manmade things, such as furniture and art. We can even see historic buildings and structures in many old cities. Most importantly, we have the memories of our oldest citizens. They are able to tell us their own stories about what life was like 100 years ago.

What happens when we attempt to study ancient history? Ancient history can be more difficult to study because of the lack of **evidence**. Scientists study the few **ruins** that remain from the past. They try to learn about the people who built them.

Few manmade objects, or **artifacts,** from ancient civilizations have survived. They become lost or destroyed over time. Weather, fire, and even people can destroy artifacts. One or two thousand years ago there were far fewer people living than today. Fewer people mean fewer artifacts.

Archaeologists photograph and record their findings.

We treasure the artifacts that we do find because they let us see into the past. By learning about the past, we begin to understand ourselves a little better. Some people spend their lives studying old buildings and artifacts so they can learn about ancient people. Professionals such as historians, **anthropologists**, and **archaeologists** work together to uncover the secrets of the past.

SPANISH INFLUENCE

Spain is part of the Iberian peninsula. A peninsula is land that is surrounded by water on three sides. Spain is located between Africa and Europe. From Spain, you can get to the Mediterranean Sea and the Atlantic Ocean. Spain has been invaded by many different armies throughout its history because of its location. Spain was also rich in gold, silver, copper, iron, and tin. These minerals and metals made Spain a target for armies looking for wealth.

*R*oman influences can be seen in Merida in western Spain.
These are the remains of a Roman theater.

Through the ages, people from many areas of the world have settled in Spain. Spanish art and buildings show signs of many cultures. Spanish art has been influenced, or affected, by the Iberians *(eye BEER ee enz)*, Celts *(SELTS)*, Romans, Basques *(BASKS),* and **Moors**. Their cultures melted into one unique Spanish style.

In more recent times, Spain has influenced styles in other parts of the world. Spain was invaded a lot, but it has also done its share of invading and exploring other lands. In fact, it was Spanish explorers that discovered America. Spain's Queen Isabella gave Italian born Christopher Columbus the ships and supplies he needed to search for a new route to India. In 1492 Columbus and his crew landed on an island in the Bahamas *(buh HAHM uhz)*. Columbus believed he had found India. Instead he had discovered America. Columbus claimed the new land for Queen Isabella and returned to Spain with the news. Columbus took a load of treasure and six natives from the New World with him.

As a reminder of Spanish influence, its worth noting that even today, after hundreds of years since the Spanish invasion, the majority of Mexicans still speak Spanish.

A palace in Seville is decorated with gold from the New World. The gold was brought to Spain by conquistadors—Spanish men who helped to take over Mexico.

Spain soon colonized America, and at one time ruled the land that is now Mexico. Hernan Cortes, a Spanish explorer, set out to conquer the land and its people. Cortes and his men marched into Tenochtitlan *(tay noch TEET lan),* the capital of the Aztec *(AZ tek)* culture. The Aztec leader, King Montezuma II, did not fear Cortes. The Spanish explorer led the Aztecs to believe he was a god. When the Aztecs learned they had been tricked by Cortes, they put up a terrific fight. It took several battles, but Cortes conquered the Aztecs.

At one time Spain was the most powerful country in Europe. Spain had colonies in North and South America. Spain grew wealthy from the gold, silver, and other treasures it received from the New World. Spain used its wealth to pay off debts from its many wars. Soon Spain's power began to fade.

This beautiful Gothic cathedral is in Segovia. Segovia is north of Madrid, Spain's capital.

PREHISTORIC ART

In 1879, a man was exploring a cave in northeast Spain, near Altamira *(ahl tuh MEE rah).* He was surprised to find large animals painted on the cave ceiling. As he moved toward the rear of the cave, he discovered more paintings and engravings on the walls. The life-like paintings were of bison, horses, and other animals. They were outlined in black and red. Now scientists have found hundreds of caves, mostly in Spain and France, that have the same kind of cave art. The paintings at Altamira are the best example.

These cave paintings were painted by artists thousands of years ago.

18

The Altamira cave paintings date back to prehistoric times. Prehistoric means before the invention of a writing system. Archaeologists and other scientists have tested the art work and proved the paintings date back to about 15,000 BC. They were created by Stone Age artists living in the **Paleolithic** period. The Paleolithic period was when humans began to use stone tools.

Ancient people made pigment, or color, by grinding different kinds of stones to a fine powder. Pigment-stained grinding stones have been found in many of the painted caves in Europe.

Why did the ancient artists paint the cave walls, and what do the paintings mean? Archaeologists have many ideas, but no one knows for sure. Perhaps they were painted to decorate the cave home, much like we paint our walls or hang pictures in our homes. They may be a part of a **ritual** to bring good fortune while hunting. Maybe the paintings tell a story, or were left as a gift from one tribe to another. We may never know why the caves were painted, but we can enjoy the prehistoric art and continue to dream up new ideas of why the walls were painted. Maybe that's what the ancient artists had in mind when they created them thousands of years ago.

The paintings at Altamira show some animals that no longer live in northern Spain. Thousands of years of climatic, or weather, changes and the impact of humans have changed Altamira, as well as many other places around the world. The changes may have forced some of the animals to die out or move to other areas.

*P*rehistoric artists used crushed stone to create the color for their paintings.

ART AND BUILDINGS

The cave paintings at Altamira and in other Spanish caves show the long history, and importance, of art to the Spanish people. Stone Age people also left other kinds of evidence that have somehow survived through the ages. Archaeologists have discovered decorated pottery and the remains of stone structures in and around Spain. Archaeologists believe Spanish pottery was first created about 2000 BC, during the **Neolithic** period.

The famous red-striped archways are in the Moorish Mosque in Cordoba.

Early Spanish people began using bronze about 1500 BC. Archaeologists call this period the Bronze Age. Making bronze is a skill that was probably brought to Spain by the Greeks. Artists created works of art out of bronze. The most famous bronze art in Spain are the great bulls' heads made during the 6th century BC. The bulls' heads are on display at a museum in Madrid *(muh DRID)*, Spain.

Roman Influence

Spain was ruled by the ancient Romans beginning about 300 BC. Many ancient Roman structures still remain in Spain. The Spanish city of Lugo is surrounded by walls built by the Romans. Other structures such as bridges and buildings also survived. A beautiful Roman **aqueduct** still brings water to the city of Segovia *(suh GO vee uh).* An aqueduct is a large stone structure that carries a small river of water to a city. An aqueduct works like underground sewer pipes that modern cities use to carry water.

Visigoth Influence

After the fall of the Roman rule, Spain was ruled for several hundred years by the Christian **Visigoths**. The Visigoths built a few churches that still remain. Their churches display primitive stone work. The biggest influence from Visigoth rule was the feeling of unity among the people living in Spain. They felt they belonged together, separate from Rome.

In the Seville Cathedral is a tomb of Christopher Columbus. It is believed that the body in the tomb is Diego, Columbus' son.

*These are remains of an ancient Roman aqueduct in Merida.
One aqueduct in Segovia is still used today.*

Moorish Influence

The Muslims were next in line to rule Spain. The Muslims were known as the Moors to the Christians. The Moors ruled parts of Spain from about AD 759 until 1492. The Moors left behind several beautiful cathedrals called **mosques**. The most famous Moorish mosque is in Cordoba *(kohr DOH bah)*. The mosque, called the Mezquita, took more than 200 years to build. The Mezquita has over 800 columns and many red-striped archways. The Moors used marble and **mosaics** in many of their structures.

While Moorish rule continued in southern Spain, northern Spain was taken over again by the Christians. The rest of Europe began to call this northern area Spain and the spoken language was called Spanish.

Spain spread south, finally taking control of the last Muslim kingdom. The Christians built one of the largest cathedrals in the world in Seville *(suh VIL)*. Treasures found in the Cathedral include a cross believed to have been made from gold that Columbus brought from the New World.

This mosaic floor is another example of Roman influence in Spain.

SPANISH GALLEONS

What comes to mind when you think of a Spanish galleon? Most people would say "treasure."

A galleon is a large ship. Galleons were used by the Spanish as warships and to haul cargo and people. Over the centuries thousands of galleons carried valuables from the New World back to Spain.

U.S.A.

FLORIDA
KEYS

BAHAMAS

Atlantic Ocean

TURKS &
CAICOS

CUBA

CAYMAN ISLANDS

PUERTO
RICO

B.V.I.

JAMAICA

HAITI

DOMINICAN
REPUBLIC

U.S.
VIRGIN ISLANDS

ST.
KITTS
NEVIS

MONT-
SERRAT

ANTIGUA &
BARBUDA

GUADELOUPE

DOMINICA

Caribbean Sea

MARTINIQUE

ST. LUCIA
ST. VINCENT

ARUBA CURAÇAO

BONAIRE

BARBADOS
THE GRENADINES
GRENADA

TOBAGO

TRINIDAD

Columbus landed in the Bahamas when searching for a new route to India.

An unusual Spanish law made it illegal for New World colonists to make many of their own products. This law kept the colonists dependent on Spain. The colonists mined silver and gold and used the treasure to pay for everything they got from the galleons. Colonies in Mexico and South America supplied Spain with huge amounts of gold and silver. Spain used the treasure in trade among other European countries.

Thousands of silver coins, gold, and other treasures were found near the wreck of the Spanish galleon Atocha.

The galleons would set out from Spain with cargo that included weapons, clothing, olive oil, and wine. After the long voyage across the Atlantic, the ships arrived at one of the many ports in the New World. The crews unloaded the cargo and reloaded the ships with gold, silver, emeralds, and other valuables. Farming products such as tobacco and sugar would also be loaded. The ships were so full and so heavy with their loads that it looked as though they would topple over under the weight.

The heavily loaded galleons were easy targets for pirates. So many galleons were lost to pirates that the ships' captains began to sail in groups of up to 150 vessels. These groups, or convoys, provided some safety against pirates. Pirates did not dare attack so many ships at once.

Storms and shallow reefs were an even greater threat to the galleons than the pirates. Hurricanes and storms separated ships sailing in convoys. Strong winds and big waves drove them off course and would often damage or sink the ships. The crew of the damaged ships were at risk of running out of fresh water and food. The captains had no choice but to land their ships as soon as they could. Stopping for food and water was risky, too. Many ships met there end after colliding with shallow reefs near land.

CHAPTER 6

SALVAGE

Spanish rulers and wealthy Spanish people needed the treasure that came from the New World. The treasure helped pay Spain's debts to other countries. It was also needed to pay for Spain's many wars. When a treasure ship was lost, it hurt Spain's economy. Wealthy people could not pay their taxes, which meant that the government could not pay its debt. Every effort was made to find the lost ships. Spain could not afford to lose the treasure.

A treasure hunter unloads a silver bar.
The silver was part of the rich treasure carried on the Atocha.

Treasure hunters use modern diving equipment when they search for shipwrecks.

Salvage means to recover or save lost treasure. Spain could not always salvage their treasure. Sometimes the sunken ships were in deep water. Many times they did not know the locations of the lost ships. The ships and their treasures, it seemed, were lost forever.

This gold cup still shines after sitting on the ocean floor for hundreds of years.

Modern treasure hunters use many ways to find and salvage ships. If the search area is in clear, shallow water, then archaeologists do a visual search first. One visual search method is to use a glass panel in the bottom of a boat. The panel is an undersea window. Other visual methods include aerial searches. Archaeologists get a bird's eye view of a large area using small planes or helicopters. Archaeologists look for underwater mounds, or other objects that might be unusual.

Once a small area is pinpointed, archaeologists do a closer search. Divers using underwater scooters comb an area looking for clues. If a ship's hull or objects such as a cannon, **ballast**, or other artifacts are found, the search team focuses on that area.

Sometimes a ship goes down in murky, or unclear, water. Even in clear water, wrecks can be covered by shifting sand. In this case, a visual search won't help. Archaeologists must use other methods to find the wreck.

TOOLS OF THE TRADE

Tens of thousands of ships have sunk to the bottom of the sea. Only a few of these ships have been found. Billions of dollars in gold, silver, and other valuables still lie hidden on the ocean floor.

Underwater archaeologists and treasure hunters use an instrument, or tool, called a **magnetometer** to help locate shipwrecks.

*This old cannon was salvaged from a sunken Spanish galleon.
Cannons were used in war and for protection from pirates.*

Proton magnetometers detect iron and steel. The tool helps scientists search for wrecks that are buried in sand or hidden by murky water. The tool is towed underwater behind a small boat. If researchers are lucky, the magnetometer will locate a ship's anchor or cannon.

A more familiar tool used by salvagers is the metal detector. Metal detectors can locate all types of metal, from small silver coins to large iron nails.

Sonar locates wrecks in deep water. Sonar is usually used to find shipwrecks in depths of 50 to 1,000 feet.

Once a shipwreck has been located, archaeologists set up a grid over the excavation site. A grid helps the divers keep track of the exact location of each found artifact. Accurate records are important. Every artifact is measured and photographed and the information is recorded so it can be studied at a later time.

Silver bars from the treasure ship Atocha are stacked after being cleaned.

A ship that has rested on the sea bottom for long periods of time doesn't look like a ship anymore. Wood timbers in the hull often break down in salt water. Sometimes all that is left are remains of the ship's cargo. Metals such as gold and silver can be found because they don't break down. Pottery, ceramics, and glassware often look as good as new. Even these items are hard to find because they can be buried under the sand.

Divers use different ways to remove the sand. One way is the prop-wash. A prop-wash uses a boat's propeller to wash away sand. Large metal pipes are placed over the propeller. The pipe directs the powerful wash, or wake, down toward the underwater work site. Sand and other sediments quickly wash away in the currents. The prop-wash method is quick and effective, but it only works in shallow water.

Another method used to remove sand is by using an airlift. An airlift works like a vacuum cleaner, sucking layers of sand and sediment up through a pipe or hose to the surface. The sand is directed into a safety screen to find small artifacts that may have been sucked up through the hose.

Deep water salvage is the most difficult. Most salvage methods are not effective at great depths. Archaeologists and treasure hunters must find new ways to salvage. New methods can be dangerous and are more costly, but for some the rewards are worth the risks.

*S*pain grew wealthy from the huge amount of gold it took from the New World.

PLACES AND NAMES PRONUNCIATION GUIDE

Places:

Altamira *(ahl tuh MEE rah)*

Bahamas *(buh HAHM uhz)*

Cordoba *(kohr DOH bah)*

Madrid *(muh DRID)*

Segovia *(suh GO vee uh)*

Seville *(suh VIL)*

Tenochtitlan *(tay noch TEET lan)*

People:

Aztec *(AZ tek)*

Basques *(BASKS)*

Celts *(SELTS)*

conquistadors *(kuhn KEES tuh dorz)*

Hernan Cortes *(air NAHN kohr TEZ)*

Iberians *(eye BEER ee enz)*

Montezuma *(mahn tuh ZOO muh)*

GLOSSARY

ancestor (AN ses ter) — a parent or relative born before you

anthropologists (AN thre POL eh jists) — people who study human origin, culture, and development

aqueduct (AK wi DUKT) — a structure used for carrying running water

archaeologist (AR kee AHL uh jest) — a person who studies past human life by studying artifacts left by ancient people

artifacts (ART eh fakts) — objects made or changed by humans

ballast (BAL est) — a heavy material used in ships to steady the ship

generation (JEN eh RAY shun) — single steps in the line of ancestors

evidence (EV e dens) — anything that can be used as proof

magnetometer (MAG ne TOM eh ter) — a tool used to measure the Earth's magnetic field

Moors (MORZ) — culture that took over Spain in the 8th century

mosaic (moe ZAY ik) — surface decorations made with small pieces of colored glass or stone

mosques (MOSKS) — buildings used by Muslims for public worship

GLOSSARY

Neolithic (NEE eh LITH ik) — a period of human
development that followed the Paleolithic period;
New Stone Age

Paleolithic (PAY lee eh LITH ik) — the earliest and longest
period of human development, lasting from about
2.5 million years ago to about 10,000 years ago;
Old Stone Age

ruins (ROO enz) — the remains of something that has
been destroyed

rituals (RICH oo elz) — a system or ceremonial way of
doing things

salvage (SAL vij) — saving a wrecked ship or its cargo

sonar (SO nar) — a method using reflected vibrations to
find things

Visigoths (VI sih goths) — people of German descent who
ruled parts of Spain in the 5th century

FURTHER READING

Spain © 1994 Andrew Eames, Houghton Mifflin Company

The Search for Sunken Treasure ©1993 Robert F. Marx and Jenifer Marx, Key Porter Books

Spain in Pictures © 1995 Lerner Publications Company

The Young Oxford Book of Archaeology ©1997 Norah Moloney, Oxford University Press, NY

Lost Treasures of the World ©1993 Michael Groushko, Multimedia Books Ltd., London

Archeology, Eyewitness Books ©1994 Dr. Jane McIntosh, Alfred A. Knopf, Inc., NY

Encarta Encyclopedia © 1996 Microsoft Corporation

Grolier Multimedia Encyclopedia ©1998 Grolier Inc.

Visigothic Spain
  www.camelotintl.com/heritage/visi.html

Shipwreck Treasures Inc.
  www.shipwrecktreasure.com/

INDEX